CELEBRATING THE
SEASONS
OF
LIFE

Mary Batchelor

A LION BOOK

Oxford · Batavia · Sydney

Text copyright © 1990 Mary Batchelor
This edition copyright © 1990 Lion Publishing

Published by
Lion Publishing plc
Sandy Lane West, Oxford, England
ISBN 0 7459 1434 9
Lion Publishing Corporation
1705 Hubbard Avenue, Batavia, Illinois 60510,
USA
ISBN 0 7459 1434 9
Albatross Books Pty Ltd
PO Box 320, Sutherland, NSW 2232, Australia
ISBN 0 7324 0150 X

First edition 1990

Sources of quotations

Pages 12–13: Song of Songs 3:11–12, Good News
Bible, copyright 1966, 1971 and 1976 American
Bible Society, published in UK by The Bible
Societies and Collins
Gerard Manley Hopkins, 'Spring'
Diary of Anne Frank, by permission of Vallentine
Mitchell & Co Ltd, London
Page 13: Algernon Charles Swinburne, 'Atalanta
in Calydon'
Pages 14–15: Dietrich Bonhoeffer, *Letters and
Papers from Prison*, by permission of William
Collins
Psalm 139:23–24, Good News Bible
St François de Sales – quoted by Jean Pierre
Camus
Page 17: Galatians 6:7–8, Good News Bible
T.S. Eliot, *The Rock*, reprinted by permission of
Faber and Faber Ltd from *Collected Poems
1909–1962*
Prayer of Chinese Christians, from *The Oxford
Book of Prayer*, ed. George Appleton
Page 18: George Macdonald, from *Thomas
Ingfold, Curate*, taken from the *George Macdonald
Anthology* by C.S. Lewis, published by Geoffrey
Bles
Moses' last words, from Deuteronomy
30:15,19–20, Good News Bible
Psalm 86:11, Good News Bible
Page 21: Christina Rossetti, 'Summer'
Page 22: 'Jamaica Market' by Agnes Maxwell-
Hall, from *Around the World in Eighty Poems*,
compiled by Jennifer and Graeme Curry, Century
Hutchinson
Samuel Taylor Coleridge, *Answer to a Child's
Question*
Pages 24–25: J.R.R. Tolkien – in conversation
Rabindranath Tagore, from *Songs of Kabir*,
translated by Rabindranath Tagore, by
permission of the Trustees of the Tagore Estate,
and Macmillan
Pages 26–27: Mother Teresa, from 'On Silence',
from *Mother Teresa's Way of Love* quoted by
Malcolm Muggeridge in *Something Beautiful for
God*, William Collins
T.S. Eliot from 'Ash Wednesday', *Collected
Poems 1909–1962*, reprinted by permission of
Faber and Faber Ltd and Harcourt Brace
Jovanovich, Orlando, Florida
Psalm 46:10

Page 29: 1 Corinthians 13:4–7, Good News Bible
1 John 4:19, Good News Bible
Catherine Bramwell-Booth, from *Letters* and
Catherine Bramwell-Booth, published by Lion
Publishing
Pages 30–31: C.S. Lewis, from *The Four Loves*,
by permission of William Collins
Proverbs 27:6, Good News Bible
Hilaire Belloc, from *Dedicatory Ode*, published by
Duckworth and A.D. Peters and Co Ltd
Page 32: Andrew Marvell, from 'To His Coy
Mistress'
Michel Quoist, from *Prayers of Life*, reprinted by
permission of Gill and MacMillan, Dublin, and
Sheed and Ward, Kansas City
Page 35: John Keats, from 'To Autumn'
Page 37: Shakespeare, from *Sonnets* (104)
Ecclesiastes 3:11, Revised Standard Version
Pages 38–39: Psalm 126:5, Good News Bible
Laurence Whistler, from 'Harvest Festival', from
The English Festivals quoted in Malcolm Saville,
Words for all Seasons, Lion Publishing, by
permission of Mr Laurence Whistler
Galatians 6:9, Good News Bible
Pages 40–41: Rainer Maria Rilke, from
'Autumn', from *Selected Works* Vol.2, *Poems*,
translated by J.B.Leishman, published by The
Hogarth Press and reprinted by permission of the
Estate of Rainer Maria Rilke and St John's
College, Oxford; USA, Rainer Rilke, 'Autumn',
Selected Poems, translated by C.F. MacIntyre by
permission of the publisher, The University of
California Press
Paul Tournier, from *Learning to Grow Old*, by
permission of the publishers – SCM Press Ltd
and Harper and Row
Clarence Winchester, 'Promise', quoted in
Malcolm Saville, *Words for All Seasons*, Lion
Publishing, by permission of Mrs Constance
Winchester
Emily Brontë, 'Fall, Leaves, Fall'
William Wordsworth, from 'Ode. Intimations of
Immortality'
Page 42: Paul Tournier, from *Learning to Grow
Old*, by permission, as above
Prayer from Singapore, from *The Oxford Book of
Prayer*
Pages 44–45: Dag Hammarskjöld, from
Markings, translated by W.H. Auden and Lief
Sjoberg, by permission of the publishers, Faber
and Faber Ltd and Alfred A. Knopf, Inc.
Psalm 46:1–3, Good News Bible
Matthew 7:24–25, Good News Bible
Page 47: Fr Trevor Huddleston, from an
interview recorded in *Drawing Near to the City* by
Shelagh Brown, published by Triangle/SPCK
Dürckheim, quoted by Paul Tournier in
Learning to Grow Old
Proverbs 9:12, Good News Bible
James 1:5, Good News Bible
Page 49: T.S. Eliot, from *A Song for Simeon*, by
permission of Faber and Faber Ltd and
Harcourt Brace Jovanovich
Pages 50–51: T.S. Eliot, from *Four Quartets*
(*East Coker*), by permission, as above
Donald Swann, from *The Space Between the
Bars*, by permission of the publisher, Hodder
and Stoughton Ltd
George Macdonald, from *Wilfred Cumbermede*
Pages 52–53: Ecclesiastes 11:7–8, Good News
Bible

1 Thessalonians 5:16,18, Good News Bible
Pages 54–55: 'As a white candle . . .' sung by
Glasgow Orpheus Choir, under Sir Hugh
Roberton
Gertrude Jekyll, from *Green Things of the Winter
Garden*, first published in *Country Life*, 29
January 1916
George Macdonald, from *Alec Forbes*, Vol.2,
Pages 56–57: Dag Hammarskjöld from
Markings, by permission, as above
St Thérèse, from *Suffering and Prayer in the Life
of St Thérèse* by Frances Hogan, Darlington
Carmel
Luke 1:78–79, Good News Bible
1 John and Psalm 36, New International
Version, copyright 1973 and 1978 New York
Bible Society
Psalm 23:4, New International Version
Pages 58–59: Dag Hammarskjöld from
Markings, by permission, as above
Arthur Koestler, from *Stranger on the Square*,
published by Hutchinson Publishing Group Ltd,
and reprinted by permission of the Peters, Fraser
and Dunlop Group Ltd
Lord Rhodes, from *My Time of Life*
2 Corinthians 4:18, Good News Bible
Luke 24:28–30, Good News Bible
Page 60: Michel Quoist, from 'I Like
Youngsters', from *Prayers of Life*, by
permission, as above
Paul Tournier, from *Learning to Grow Old*, by
permission, as above

Photographs
Sonia Halliday and Laura Lushington
Photographs/Sister Daniel, pages 35, 38 (right),
39 (right); Lion/David Alexander, pages 16, 38
(left), 39 (centre and left), 40 (right)/David
Townsend, cover (except centre right and
bottom left), pages 5, 7 (top and centre top), 15,
21, 26, 38 (centre), 40 (left), 45, 56 (both)/Jon
Willcocks, page 7 (centre bottom); Sheila
Robinson, page 7 (bottom); Zefa (UK) Ltd,
cover (centre right and bottom left), pages 8, 11,
12 (both), 13 (both), 14, 19, 22, 23, 25, 26/27,
28, 30, 31, 33, 36, 41 (both), 43, 44, 46, 49, 50
(both), 52, 53, 55, 57 (both), 59, 61

**British Library Cataloguing in Publication
Data**
Batchelor, Mary
Celebrating the seasons of life.
1. Christian life
I. Title
248.4

ISBN 0 7459 1434 9

**Library of Congress Cataloging-in-Publication
Data**
(applied for)

Printed in Spain

Contents

Introduction

Spring

Summer

Autumn

Winter

Introduction

Most of us live in lands where every season brings its own particular character. Suddenly, or by slow degrees, cold gives way to heat, dryness to rainfall, and new life bursts forth where there has been deadness and decay.

Human life has its seasons, too. Youth has the vitality and newness of spring. Full, busy years follow, with a summer warmth and abundance of life at work and in the family. In the autumn of middle life there is some falling off in commitments and strength, and a time to enjoy the harvest of earlier years. Winter, like old age, brings a slowing of activity, yet there is continued growth, even though it may be hidden from sight.

The seasons fall at different times for different people, so in this book no age-limits are prescribed. Some have a short spring. Others experience the restrictions of winter, through disability or bereavement, at an early age, while their contemporaries still bask in the sunshine of summer or autumn. A few may be grandparents at forty while others of the same age are eagerly awaiting the arrival of their first child. But all of us, early or late, are likely to experience the characteristics of every season.

The seasons themselves do not always run true to form. There may be mild and sunny days in winter, and storms in midsummer. In life, the experiences and emotions we associate with one period occur at other stages too. There are some questions that must be asked again and again as each new season comes. At every age we need to discover who we are and where our lives are going. At every age we need to go on growing as human beings, searching and discovering the truth about our world, ourselves and about God.

So, in the pages that follow, some of the experiences linked to one season may also belong to another. But, for the most part, each season contains the situations and responses that match the spring, summer, autumn and winter of life. In this way we may learn to appreciate the characteristic beauty of every season and draw upon the richness and benefits that each can bring to us.

MARY BATCHELOR

SPRING

Spring is the season of planting and sowing, of new growth and new beginnings. It is a time of vigour and freshness. In the springtime of life we are young and newly independent. We have thrown off the restraints of childhood and teen years. We are free to set our own goals and make our own choices. The whole of life stretches ahead. We look forward to the expansiveness of summer. Autumn and winter are far away.

New Life – New Freedom

" Nothing is so beautiful as Spring
When weeds, in wheels, shoot long and lovely and lush. "

GERARD MANLEY HOPKINS

" I looked out of the open window too, over a large area of Amsterdam,
over all the roofs and on to the horizon, which was such a pale blue
that it was hard to see the dividing line. 'As long as this exists,' I
thought, 'and I may live to see it, this sunshine, the cloudless skies, while
this lasts, I cannot be unhappy.' "

FROM THE DIARY OF ANNE FRANK

There is a very special pleasure in new things. Even when we were children we loved new clothes, a fresh clean exercise book or shiny new toys. That pleasure in new things stays with us. Spring is the season of newness and we respond to it with hope and happiness. With the first taste of life as independent men and women, all the freshness of spring is ours to enjoy. We glory in new powers, new status, new freedoms. We begin a new kind of life, whether we stay at home or move to another town or country.

We acquire knowledge and learn new skills, find new pursuits to enjoy. We make new relationships and friendships too.

There is a sense of heady intoxication at the prospect of so much that is new in our lives. Yet, at the same time, one part of us is often nervous and uncertain when we leave the security of the world we know – our school, or home, or community.

" The winter is over; the rains
have stopped; in the countryside
the flowers are in bloom. This
is the time for singing. "

FROM SONG OF SONGS

At any stage of life, welcoming the new need not mean abandoning the old. It is good to keep old and trusted friends and to maintain strong family ties. Firm and well-founded beliefs, which we have made our own, can also provide a secure base and clear guidelines to steer us in new paths. Recognizing the things that are really important to us will enable us to make the most of new opportunities and greater freedoms.

" Blossom by blossom the spring begins. "
SWINBURNE

13

Discovering Myself

" Who am I? This or the other?
Am I one person today, and tomorrow another?
Am I both at once? A hypocrite before others,
and before myself a contemptibly woebegone weakling?...
Who am I? They mock me, these lonely questions of mine.
Whoever I am, thou knowest, O God, I am thine. **"**

DIETRICH BONHOEFFER,
LETTERS AND PAPERS FROM PRISON

"Know thyself" were the words written in the ancient temple of Delphi. But it is only when we become mature that we are able to arrive at a balanced estimate of ourselves. While we were growing up, it was other people – our parents, our teachers and our friends – who defined for us the kind of people we were.

The teenage years are often full of anxiety and doubt. We ask ourselves: "Am I normal?" or "Will anyone love me?"

But once we are adult we are able to take a more realistic look at ourselves. The worst insecurities of adolescence are behind us. Now is the time to assess our weaknesses and strengths as honestly as we can. If we are to grow, we need to understand what makes us tick.

Honesty with ourselves helps us to understand others better too. We are less likely to be critical if we are aware of our own contradictory feelings and motives. We are more likely to feel

" Examine me, O God, and know my mind;
test me, and discover my thoughts.
Find out if there is any evil in me
and guide me in the everlasting
way. **"** FROM PSALM 139

compassion when we recognize our own capacity to feel anger, love, or grief.

❝ Be patient with everyone, but above all with yourself. I mean, do not be disheartened by your imperfections... How are we to be patient in bearing with our neighbour's faults, if we are impatient in bearing with our own? He who is fretted by his own failings, will not correct them; all profitable correction comes from a calm, peaceful mind. ❞

ST FRANÇOIS DE SALES

Planting and Sowing

Do not deceive yourselves; no one makes a fool of God. A person will reap exactly what he sows. If he sows in the field of his natural desires, from it he will gather the harvest of death; if he sows in the field of the Spirit, from the Spirit he will gather the harvest of eternal life.

FROM GALATIANS 6

When the farmer looks at the brown fields, he sees, in prospect, the crop that will one day ripen there. So it is in hope that he sows his seed and works hard during the months that separate sowing time from harvest.

When we are young we also plan for a chosen harvest. Some set out to make a million before they are thirty, some to reach the top of their chosen profession. Others work towards a future of marriage, home and family. Many would like both!

We may reach these particular goals but that is not the only harvest we shall reap. Success is not finally measured in terms of money, prestige or even personal fulfilment. In a single-minded attempt to get what we want, it is dangerously easy to lose sight of everything and everyone else.

Take no thought of harvest But only of proper sowing. T.S. ELIOT

If we ignore the needs and feelings of other people, if we neglect the spiritual dimension to life, these attitudes too will bring their inevitable result. We may not have bargained for this kind of harvest, but we need to sow wisely with regard to human relationships and to God if we are to reap a reward in this field too.

I pray thee, Lord, to sow the good seed of virtue in my heart and make it grow by day and night and bring forth a hundredfold.

PRAYER OF CHINESE CHRISTIANS

Choices

" When people seek advice it is often in the hope of finding the adviser side with their second familiar self instead of their awful first self of which they know so little. "
GEORGE MACDONALD

" Today I am giving you a choice between good and evil, between life and death... Choose life. Love the Lord your God, obey him and be faithful to him. "
MOSES' LAST WORDS TO THE PEOPLE OF ISRAEL

When my children were younger, the highlight of their birthdays was being allowed to choose – what to have to eat, what friends to invite, what games to play.

One of the pleasures of growing up and reaching the age of independence is that we are free to choose, not just on birthdays but any day of the year, to be responsible at last for our own way of life.

We are free to decide what training to take, what job to look for, where to live.

" The more alternatives, the more difficult the choice. " ABBÉ D'ALLAINVAL

Not everyone is fortunate enough to have these choices. There may be no jobs to be had or it may be necessary to take any work that is offered. But there are many other areas in which to choose. We can decide how to spend our money, how to use our leisure time, what interests or activities to take up.

Making choices is not always easy. We may be confused by the number of options on offer or be afraid of taking the wrong option. A friend used to say that, out of every three decisions we make, one will probably be right, another wrong, and the third will not matter either way! That can be some comfort!

" It is one thing to see the land of peace from a wooded ridge... and another to tread the road that leads to it. "
ST AUGUSTINE

But it is even better to recognize that God promises to guide and lead us if we ask him to. Like the best kind of father, he wants what is good for us and will help us to make wise decisions. When we make mistakes he is ready to forgive and get us back on the right path.

Some of the choices made at this stage have far-reaching effects. But in many cases they are short term. We can afford to make a few mistakes. We have not yet arrived at the summer of life, when we must settle more seriously to our life work and relationships.

" Teach me, Lord, what you want me to do, and I will obey you faithfully. "
PSALM 86

SUMMER

" *Summer days for me*
When every leaf is on its tree. "
CHRISTINA ROSSETTI

Summer is the season of warmth, abundance and fulfilment.
It can also be hot and exhausting.
In the summer of life we live at full stretch — at home, at
work and in the community — enjoying the richness of life.
Time presses: yet we need to make space for rest,
for relaxation and for reflection.
Now is also the opportunity to weigh the options still open to
us, and to negotiate change, where it is appropriate, while we can.

Living at High Noon

> **"** Mangoes, breadfruit, ginger-roots,
> Granadillas, bamboo-shoots,
> Cho-cho, ackees, tangerines,
> Lemons, purple Congo-beans,
> Sugar, okras, kola-nuts,
> Citrons, hairy coconuts...
> Black skin, babel – and the sun
> That burns all colours into one. **"** AGNES MAXWELL-HALL, JAMAICA MARKET

In summer, life is at its richest. There is sunshine, warmth, flowers – an abundance of sound and colour.

The summer season of life is often rich and colourful too. So much is happening all at once, in the family, at work and at leisure, with friends and with colleagues.

At this stage of life we sometimes take the fulness and richness for granted. We may even complain of too much to do. It is hard to believe that life will not always be like this.

But summer will gradually give place to autumn and winter, the quieter seasons of life. The plenty and variety of the present is to be relished while it it is with us.

Later years will bring their own pleasures and fulfilment. But we will never again have such a time to enjoy – when we are at the height of our powers and deeply involved with people and activities. So summer is the time for celebration!

> **"** Green leaves, and blossoms,
> And warm sunny weather,
> And singing and loving –
> All come back together **"**
> SAMUEL TAYLOR COLERIDGE

> **"** Here is God's plenty. **"** OLD PROVERB

Who Am I Now?

" 'The common round, the daily task'... which furnish so much more than one actually asks. "

J.R.R. TOLKIEN

" POSITION VACANT: HOUSEWIFE *Applications are invited for the position of manager of a lively team of four demanding individuals of differing needs and personalities. The successful applicant will be required to perform and co-ordinate the following functions: companion, counsellor, financial manager, buying officer, teacher, nurse, chef, nutritionist, decorator, cleaner, driver, child care supervisor, social secretary and recreation officer.*
Hours of work: all waking hours and a twenty-four hour shift when necessary.
Pay: none. " FROM A BOOKLET PRODUCED BY THE NSW WOMEN'S ADVISORY COUNCIL

" I laugh when I hear that the fish in the water is thirsty.
You wander restlessly from forest to forest while the Reality is within your own dwelling.
The truth is here!
Go where you will –
to Benares or to Mathura;
until you have found God in your own soul, the whole world will seem meaningless to you. "

RABINDRANATH TAGORE

"Am I anything more than the roles I play?" That is often the question we find ourselves asking at the end of a busy day filled with one call after another on our time and energy. It's a struggle to meet all the demands made on us as parents and children, as home makers and marriage partners, let alone our commitment in the world of work. What room is left to be ourselves?

Yet we *are* more than robots, programmed to fulfil certain functions and do certain tasks. We are individual people with our own human needs.

One day, we shall no longer be needed as we are now. It will be fatal then, as it is foolish now, to live at the mercy of life's demands. It is not selfish to try to retain our individuality. We are not being kind to those we serve when we allow them to take us over. If we think we are indispensable at our job, we are denying others the chance to prove themselves. When caring for family and home becomes our sole preoccupation, we do our loved ones a disservice. They need to learn some independence too.

It is important to allow ourselves time to develop and grow as people in our own right. We need emotional and spiritual space in order to draw strength for the roles we are called on to play. Self-sacrifice may be required if we are to serve others lovingly and well. But we are not meant to be puppets on a string. Our

self-giving has to flow from a resolved and willing commitment.
Then we shall discover that selfless love brings its own reward.

Give up yourself and you will find your real self Submit to death,
death of your ambitions and favourite wishes every day, and death of
your whole body in the end. Submit with every fibre of your being.
Keep nothing back. Nothing that you have not given away will ever be
really yours.
C.S. LEWIS

The Heat of a Summer's Day

" Build into your day little enclosures of silence; they spill over into your life, bringing peace, the peace of God. "

" We need to find God and he cannot be found in noise and restlessness. God is the friend of silence... the more we receive in silent prayer, the more we can give in our active life. " MOTHER TERESA

So many things to do! So many people to see! So many decisions to make! Summer brings abundance, the warmth of plenty and fulfilment at work and home. But it brings pressures too. Even where there are resources and energy to meet the demands, there are also times of staleness and exhaustion. If we are to survive the summer heat we must set aside time for rest and refreshment.

Rest need not mean inactivity. Exercise is a great restorer of mind as well as body. A quiet walk or an energetic game of tennis, swimming or a work-out in the gym – the choice can be made to suit our own needs and opportunities.

We all cherish our particular dream of a break from routine. A harassed mother's idea of bliss may be to relax for ten minutes in a warm bath. Some feel refreshed by taking time to stand still and drink in the loveliness of the country or the busyness of the world around. Others listen to music, read, or watch a favourite programme.

Small oases of quiet and refreshment are necessary – and

*" Teach us to care and not to care
Teach us to sit still. "* T.S. ELIOT

possible – for almost all of us, if we take as much trouble to make space for them as we do to plan our usual work.

Our minds need refreshment too. Those who are stretched to capacity in their daily work need to allow their minds to relax. People in routine jobs, or caring for children, require mental stimulus. Contrast is what counts, for a change is as good as a rest.

In the summer time of life we need spiritual refreshment too. When we pause to be still during a busy day we can recognize God's presence, wherever we may be. It's through such moments of quietness that we find strength to endure the summer's heat.

❝ Be still, and know that I am God. ❞   PSALM 46

❝ O God, make us children of quietness and heirs of peace. ❞
ST CLEMENT, FIRST CENTURY AD

27

The Gift of Love

" Love is patient and kind; it is not jealous or conceited or proud; love is not ill-mannered or selfish or irritable... Love never gives up. **"**
FROM 1 CORINTHIANS 13

" Someone would like to have you for her child
But you are mine.
Someone would like to rear you on a costly mat
But you are mine.
Someone would like to place you on a camel blanket
But you are mine.
I have you to rear on a torn old mat.
Someone would like to have you as her child
But you are mine. **"**
LULLABY, THE AKAN PEOPLE OF AFRICA

The summer season of life is often rich in loving relationships – with life partner, children and parents, as well as the wider network of relatives and close friends.

But these are busy days and it is easy to take love and loved ones for granted. Yet if love is to survive and flourish it must be fostered and nourished by kindness, care and precious time.

Learning to love requires a lifetime of practice. It involves thinking of the good of the loved one rather than standing on our own rights. It means being ready to give to the utmost limit. But to love is not to indulge. We need to be firm as well as gentle, to discipline our children. We must be honest as well as kind to one another and give time to listen to the other's point of view.

Some experience the breakdown of loving relationships during these years. It is easy to react by withdrawing into ourselves. We don't want to risk being hurt a second time. But unless we make ourselves vulnerable and go out in love and care towards others, we shall miss the true purpose of life.

" Although I conquer all the earth,
Yet for me there is only one city.
In that city there is for me only
one house;
And in that house, one room only;
And in that room, a bed.
And one woman sleeps there,
The shining joy and jewel of my
kingdom. **"**
ANCIENT INDIA

" We love because God first loved us. **"**
FROM 1 JOHN 4

" Pray for love. It is a fire – feed it – fan it. Neglected, it will soon die out. Stir it up by exercise every day... Guard it from the stifling atmosphere of selfishness. Self-seeking will extinguish it before you realize what has happened, and then you will be changed. **"**
CATHERINE BRAMWELL-BOOTH

Rich in Friends

"In a circle of true Friends each man is simply what he is: stands for nothing but himself... He is lucky beyond desert to be in such company. Especially when the whole group is together, each bringing out all that is best, wisest, or funniest in all the others. Those are the golden sessions; when four or five of us after a hard day's walking have come to our inn; when our slippers are on, our feet spread out towards the blaze and our drinks at our elbows... Life – natural life – has no better gift to give. Who could have deserved it?"

C.S. LEWIS

"A friend means well even when he hurts you."

FROM THE BOOK OF PROVERBS

Every season of life can justly celebrate friendship. From the day when a child proudly brings home "my best friend", to old age, friends bring us richness, strength and happiness.

Some men and women are fortunate to find the dearest of all friends in a marriage partner; others keep close, lifelong ties of friendship with brothers and sisters and other members of their family.

But even the happiest married person needs a wider circle of friends too. C.S. Lewis, in *The Four Loves*, laments the fact that friendship is undervalued in our day. He writes about the strong bond of friendship between men, but women too find comradeship, comfort and mental stimulus in friendship with other women.

"From quiet homes and first beginning,
Out to the undiscovered ends,
There's nothing worth the wear of winning,
But laughter and the love of friends."

HILAIRE BELLOC

Friendship has been overshadowed by romantic love. Sadly, where genuine, close friendships exist, onlookers may assume a sexual relationship too. Friendship has been neglected and tarnished – all the more reason to restore it to its rightful place.

When we reach the summer season of life we have had time to know and prove our friends. But, in the rush and busyness of work and family life, we may easily neglect them. There doesn't seem to be time any more for those leisurely walks and talks, or the shared meals we once enjoyed. The hallmark of true friendship is that we can begin again, just where we left off, however long the absence. But when friendship is not nourished and enjoyed, our lives are poorer.

A friend may delightfully share my way of looking at life, so that we can explore ideas or discuss people and events with perfect understanding. We can laugh at the same jokes. Or, on the contrary, a friend may be my complete opposite, showing me a new and stimulating angle from which to view the world.

A friend is utterly trustworthy, will not betray my confidences or dismiss my fears as groundless. A friend is truthful, knowing and loving me well enough to tell me when I am wrong.

Friends stand alongside, sharing and enjoying and enriching life for one another. Friendship is best celebrated by valuing our friends at their true worth.

" Shang ya!
I want to be your friend
for ever and ever without break
or decay.
When the hills are all flat
And the rivers are all dry,
When it lightens and thunders
in winter,
When it rains and snows in summer,
When heaven and Earth mingle –
Not till then will I part from you. "
ANONYMOUS, FROM CHINA, FIRST CENTURY

Time Flies

One day we wake up to the fact that we shan't be young – not *really* young – much longer. And we still haven't done half the things we promised ourselves. Now is the time to take stock, to examine our ambitions and ideals again and to take action where it is needed.

Some things will not wait. If we want to settle down and have a family we must do so soon or miss the chance.

We may have unfulfilled ambitions at work. Now could be the time to train for new skills. We may decide to move out of a large city into the country or apply for a job overseas.

It is important to take definite steps, when we can, to satisfy our deep needs. We may have to take risks, and we may not always succeed, but we shall have the satisfaction of knowing that we have made every effort to achieve our goals.

On the other hand, we may not be free to act as we please. Too many other people depend on us. For their sakes we have to keep to our present pattern of life. But it is still important to look again at our cherished ambitions and come to terms with our disappointment or sadness.

It is important to give up our unrealized ambitions as a voluntary act. If we face disappointment and frustration in this positive way we leave no foothold for bitterness or destructive self-pity. We shall find strength and courage to accept and welcome the opportunities for fulfilment that we already enjoy. Instead of looking back, we shall look forward to the good things life has to offer in the years ahead.

" But at my back I always hear Time's wingèd chariot hurrying near. "
ANDREW MARVELL

" Time and tide wait for no one. "
ANCIENT PROVERB

" Lord, I have time,
I have plenty of time,
All the time that you give me,
The years of my life,
The days of my years,
The hours of my days,
They are all mine.
Mine, to fill, quietly, calmly,
But to fill completely, up to the brim,
To offer them to you...
I am not asking you tonight, Lord, for time to do this and then that,
But your grace to do conscientiously, in the time that you give me, what you want me to do. "
MICHEL QUOIST

32

$\mathcal{A}$UTUMN

"*Season of mists and mellow fruitfulness.*"
JOHN KEATS

Autumn is the time of harvest. It is a mild and mellow season,
but gales may come, warning of winter's approach.
In middle life, as summer gives way to autumn, we begin to reap
the harvest of the goals we set in the first half of life. But there is
still time to sow for a second harvest. Storms may warn of coming
loss and our own mortality. We carry the responsibility now,
as the older generation.

Autumn Shades

*" Beauteous spring's to yellow autumn turn'd
In process of the seasons. "*
                                        WILLIAM SHAKESPEARE

*" He has made everything beautiful in its time; also he has put eternity
into man's mind. "*
                                        FROM ECCLESIASTES 3

Autumn has a richness and beauty all its own. For every simple colour of spring or summer, autumn has a subtle range of hues, some delicate, others bold and vivid. Green leaves are still to be seen but other trees and plants are a riot of yellow, scarlet, crimson, russet and brown.

The autumn of life brings a new and subtle beauty to men and women too. The simple beauty of youth gives place to the more sophisticated attraction of maturity.

We have grown rich through experience in many areas of life. We have acquired knowledge and skills, and come to understand human nature.

We have been enriched by friendships and loving relationships.

We have discovered that we can laugh at ourselves rather than at others.

We have learned hard lessons through suffering and sadness, as well as experiencing joy.

We have laughed and cried, and our humanity has been deepened.

We have a wealth of varied memories too. We are more able to see the present in perspective because we have lived through the past.

We are also young enough to be rich in prospects. We can still look forward – to new enjoyments and new experiences that lie in the future.

Here is subtlety and richness, as varied as our individual experiences of life have been. Let us celebrate our wealth – in love and friendship, experience and knowledge; in treasured memories of the past and bright hopes for the future.

Harvest and Thanksgiving Time

*" Let those who wept as they sowed their seed,
Gather the harvest with joy. "*

FROM PSALM 126

*" Blood-dark dahlias, bronze corn-coloured chryanthemums, mauve
Michaelmas daisies — these are the flowers that wrangle with the
loud saints above them in hot-coloured jubilation... Around the font,
and along the window ledges, and each side of the chancel steps, there
are pools and tumuli of apples, melons, plums and peaches; potatoes,
turnips and cucumbers; baskets of figs, currants, raspberries and nuts;
great dropsical marrows; and loaves of bread confessing to sheaves. "*

LAURENCE WHISTLER, HARVEST FESTIVAL

Autumn is the season for reaping what was sown in spring and summer. It is the time of Thanksgiving, when we look back on the past and count our blessings. In life, too, we reach a time when we begin to enjoy the benefits of earlier years of work and effort. We can look back on much that has been good and positive and give thanks with happiness for the fruit of earlier years that we are enjoying now.

It is good when early goals have been achieved.

We may recognize the harvest in a marriage that has survived difficulties and grown stronger.

We may feel satisfaction that we supported and helped our

parents when they needed us, or that our children have been successfully launched in life.

But some see fewer satisfactions for the years of hope and hard work.

We may get little reward in our work.

We may be coping with a broken marriage, or with children who disregard our advice and seem to reject our love for them.

The harvest then seems a bitter one.

It is important to ask, again, what we mean by success. If we measure it solely in terms of money, status or self-fulfilment, we may indeed have little to show for our efforts. But true success is more than this. If we have sown well, in terms of loving and giving; in putting God and others first; in investing our best into all that we have done, there *will* be a harvest, even if we do not see it now.

❝ *Let us not become tired of doing good; for if we do not give up, the time will come when we will reap the harvest.* **❞**   FROM GALATIANS 6

The Leaves are Falling

" The leaves are falling, falling as from far,
as though above were withering farthest gardens;
they fall with a denying attitude...

We are all falling. This hand's falling too —
all have this falling-sickness none withstands.

And yet there's One whose gently-holding hands
this universal falling can't fall through. "

RAINER MARIA RILKE

" You can still live intensely... If there is a 'minus' there is also a 'plus'...
one loses something only to acquire something else... an aspect of life
which could not be known before. "

DR PAUL TOURNIER

In many lands trees lose their leaves when autumn comes. In life we often suffer similar loss. Parents grow old and die; children leave home; death or desertion may bring marriage to an end. At work there can be loss of power or prestige, as younger colleagues overtake us.

It is natural to grieve for the losses we experience, but time will bring new opportunities. When we have shed the roles and responsibilities of younger days, we are free to be truly ourselves.

" Autumn has come again;
the falling leaves
Are shed as old men's years, and
drift away. "   CLARENCE WINCHESTER

We can express our own creativity and usefulness in ways of our own choosing.

We have been stripped bare of relationships, of responsibility, or of the busyness of life, but the trunk and branches of our true self remain. We can once more be people in our own right. We shall discover fresh outlets for our energies and find joy again in serving God and one another in new ways.

❝ I do not know how or when it may please God to give you the quiet of mind that you need, but I believe it is to be had, and in the meantime you must go on doing your work, trusting God even for this. ❞

GEORGE MACDONALD

❝ Fall, leaves, fall;
die, flowers, away;
Lengthen night and shorten day;
Every leaf speaks bliss to me
Fluttering from the autumn tree. ❞

EMILY BRONTË

❝ Though nothing can bring back the hour
Of splendour in the grass,
of glory in the flower;
We will grieve not, rather find
Strength in what remains behind. ❞

WILLIAM WORDSWORTH

Autumn Ploughing

When the farmer has harvested the corn, he straight away begins to plough the land, preparing it for the next crop. Midlife is the time when we reap the results of our earlier actions, but it is also a time to plough and prepare our lives for a second sowing.

If the harvest of the first half of life has been rewarding, we cannot rest at that. Now is the time to set new goals and plan for future profit.

Sometimes, when we seem to have reaped nothing but disappointment and dissatisfaction, we have to admit that it is because we sowed the wrong kind of seed. We may have planned only in terms of outward success and personal satisfaction. We may have neglected marriage and family or, worse, left God out of our life. The present is the inevitable result of the past.

There is still time to sow for a second harvest. But ploughing comes first and that may not be easy or pleasant. We have to take stock of the years that have passed, rethinking long-held attitudes and examining motives. We may need to bring to the surface memories that we would rather forget.

We must deal with the past, so that it does not spoil the future. Grudges and resentments must be admitted and then laid to rest.

We must confess to our own mistakes and selfishness too.

We need to ask forgiveness from God, as well as from those we have wronged.

And then we need to forgive ourselves.

When we have ploughed thoroughly we can begin to sow again, perhaps more wisely and for a more enduring harvest.

When the Wind Blows

*"Fading beeches, bright against
A dark storm-cloud.
Wind rips up the forest-pond's
Steel-grey water... Silence shatters to pieces
The mind's armour
Leaving it naked before
Autumn's clear eye."*

DAG HAMMARSKJÖLD

*"God is our shelter and strength,
always ready to help in times of trouble.
So we will not be afraid, even if the earth is shaken...
even if the seas roar and rage,
and the hills are shaken by the violence."*

FROM PSALM 46

Autumn may be sunny and mild, but it can also be the time when storms and hurricanes suddenly strike. At this time in life too, tragedy and disaster can come to us out of a blue sky.

Even when the events of life shake us to the very depths, our life need not collapse in ruins. The secret of survival is trust in God, who cannot be shaken.

Sometimes people say that they have lost their faith, because of some tragedy that has come to them or to someone they love.

Perhaps that faith had no real foundation, but was only an outward form of words and religion.

Jesus said that the person who can survive the tempests and storms of life is the one who obeys his teaching, as well as trusting in his love.

When trouble comes, such trust will steady the heart and mind in reliance upon God.

However firm our faith, we all need time to recover from the shock of sudden disaster. We must allow time to grieve for what has been lost and come to terms with new, changed situations.

During that period we may suffer from doubt, depression or fear. But when God is the foundation of our life, we *shall* survive the storm. In time he will create something new and worthwhile out of seeming devastation and destruction.

Jesus said: **"** *Anyone who hears these words of mine and obeys them is like a wise man who built his house on rock. The rain poured down, the rivers overflowed, and the wind blew hard against that house. But it did not fall, because it was built on rock.* **"**   FROM MATTHEW 7

The Age of Wisdom?

"It is true that sometimes as one gets older one also gets wiser and therefore more able to help people because of one's own experience and because of the joys and the sorrows one has had in one's life."

FR TREVOR HUDDLESTON

"Hardening... bitterness... a withdrawn and uncommunicative character, are the signs of human non-maturity."

DÜRCKHEIM

When our parents and aunts and uncles die, it comes as a shock to us to realize that we are now the older generation. However young we may feel, we are the new leaders.

We shall not behave as our parents did. We may not expect the younger generation to follow our lead. But by being ourselves – loving or self-centred, critical or accepting, good-natured or irritable – we are modelling for them the image of the older generation.

Being old and being wise do not necessarily go together.

Most of us will have acquired knowledge, skills and understanding of life in many ways.

But true wisdom goes deeper. It describes, among other things, the character of the person who sees life in true perspective and who makes decisions and faces crises in a positive and fruitful way.

Socrates said that the person with least wisdom is the one who makes the greatest claim to be wise. So if we don't *feel* wise that can be a healthy sign. When we are honest about our lack of wisdom we may be humble enough to ask for help.

"You are the one who will profit if you have wisdom, and if you reject it, you are the one who will suffer."

FROM PROVERBS 9

"If any of you lacks wisdom, he should pray to God, who will give it to him; because God gives generously and graciously to all."

FROM JAMES 1

$\mathcal{W}$ INTER

" The winter sun creeps by the snow hills. "
T.S. ELIOT

Winter closes in around us. It restricts, yet the narrowing of
possibilities offers its own special bonus of satisfaction. The earth
may be cold and still, but there is warmth and growth within.
In our own season of winter, we shed the restraints and ties
of earlier years, and we can enjoy a new expansion of spirit. In old
age, we can experience secret growth, and the warmth of kindness
and love, received and given.

Free at Last!

"Our moments of happiness are those when we see a burning light through the bars of our personal prison, when for some amazing reason we look out through the cracks; or perhaps by suffering with someone in charity, we leap out of the prison itself, guided by the Spirit... the grace of God is shaped in my mind like a key, that comes from time to time and unlocks the heavy doors."

DONALD SWANN

"We die daily. Happy those who daily come to life as well."

GEORGE MACDONALD

It's good to come indoors, after a morning's shopping, and put down the loaded bags that have been straining at our muscles. As we shed our outdoor clothes and heavy shoes, we breathe a sigh of relief.

The winter of life is a time of loss – loss of loved ones, of employment, of the sharpness of our senses. But loss can bring freedom. We rightly shed the burdens of earlier years and can sigh with relief at our new-found freedoms.

No need now to worry about our image.

We need no longer fit the pattern prescribed by our former roles in life.

We can exchange our formal suits for comfortable clothes of our own choosing.

We can even afford to be a little eccentric. Does it matter if we talk to ourselves, or sing in the supermarket?

❝ When I am an old woman I shall wear purple,
With a red hat that doesn't go and doesn't suit me.
I shall sit down on the pavement when I'm tired.
And run my stick along the public railings
And make up for the sobriety of my youth. ❞

Best of all, we can be free from the tyranny of time. After years of keeping to fixed hours of work and leisure, of regulated mealtimes and bedtime, we can now create our own patterns.

Sleep may be hard to come by, but there is no need to lie awake half the night. If we choose, we can go to bed late, get up early, or listen to the radio in the small hours.

There is time to talk, to listen, to help others.

There is opportunity to do the things we never had time to do before.

It may be too late to climb mountains or learn to ski, but there are numberless other options, appropriate to our age.

It is never too late to learn – formally at college, or through reading and studying at home.

We can acquire new skills, from the practical to the creative. On a recent visit to a housing community for the elderly, I met one man who had taken up painting after retirement and is now proficient in oils and water colour. Another inmate uses her skill in flower arranging to keep the communal living-room beautiful.

But not all of us enjoy such freedom.

Old age can bring severe restrictions and loss of independence.

It is hard to feel that we are free when others choose for us and lay down the pattern for our lives.

Yet, down the ages, men and women who have had their freedom taken from them have learned that they can still enjoy inner freedom. They discover that, even when the body is confined, the mind and spirit can go free.

Jesus promises his followers that the freedom he gives will make us *really* free.

❝ Old men ought to be explorers
Here and there does not matter
We must be still and still moving
Into another intensity ❞   T.S. ELIOT

❝ Old Uncle Luke he thinks
he's cute
But Grandpa's even cuter;
He's ninety-eight and stays
out late
With Grandma on her scooter. ❞

A BOY OF EIGHT

Warmth in
Winter

" Soon, the sun will penetrate our cell, so that we can see again for ourselves that the Good God never forgets us. He showers sunlight, food and drink on everyone, the good and bad alike... I am even now amazed how quietly the sun comes to us... I would like to extend my brotherly greetings to the newly discovered particles of dust, hated here by everyone, in gratitude for their willingness to stay with us so quietly and inconspicuously... See how the dust glitters! No doubt the ability to see this way is a precious grace because our eyes suddenly see the rays of the invisible world. "

FATHER LIZNA, WHO SERVED MANY YEARS IN PRISON FOR HIS FAITH

" It is good to be able to enjoy the pleasant light of day. Be grateful for every year you live. " FROM ECCLESIASTES 11

There is nothing so cosy and comfortable as being indoors, in the warm, when the wind is blowing or the snow falling.

People who are loving and giving are warm people whose influence is most clearly felt when they themselves have reached the winter of life. They bring a lifetime's store of loving, unhurried warmth to everyone whose lives they touch.

I once visited a home for retired Salvation Army officers and met Christian men and women who had spent their lives in poverty, hard work and self-giving.

They were happy, smiling people, still giving to one another, to those who cared for them, and to all who came to the house.

Thankfulness is another kind of giving. I have a friend, in her eighties, who always finds something to be thankful for.

"The more you thank God," she says, "the more you find to thank him for." Her smile and her words radiate warmth to us all.

Those who love to give must also learn to take. Some who are too proud to receive, find it hard to grow old with grace and cheerfulness.

"We are all beggars before God," Martin Luther said.

When we learn, humbly, to receive from God the gifts he offers, of forgiveness, peace and strength, we may be readier to take from others too. In giving and receiving we open ourselves to one another and experience the warmth of love.

❝ *Grandmothers have nothing to do, they only have to be there. If they take you for a walk, they go slowly past beautiful things like leaves and caterpillars. They never say 'Come on quickly' or 'Hurry up for goodness' sake'... When they read to us they don't leave out anything. They do not mind if it's always the same story... Grandmothers are the only grown-ups who always have time.* **❞**

A SMALL GIRL, WRITING ABOUT GRANDPARENTS

❝ *It is in giving that we receive, It is in pardoning that we are pardoned.* **❞**   ST FRANCIS OF ASSISI

❝ *Be joyful always... be thankful in all circumstances.* **❞**

FROM 1 THESSALONIANS 5

Old is Beautiful

Most of us, when we grow old, lose the physical beauty we once had. But an old face can have a loveliness of its own, which is the result not of nature but of character. As I grow older, my face becomes mine to make beautiful or ugly.

Beauty in an older person can be seen in the lines that life has etched on the face. Sadness and joy, success and failure, endurance and anxiety all make their mark. But experience does not automatically beautify. When, instead of softening and enlarging the soul, it hardens and embitters, the effects are just as clearly visible.

The face mirrors the character. The set of the mouth and jaw, the glance of the eye, all reflect lifelong habits. Gentleness, tolerance, thankfulness, compassion and unselfconscious concern for others can be discerned in the face. The peace and knowledge of God leave their mark of beauty too.

Thousands of years ago a wise man wrote:

"Being cheerful keeps you healthy. It is slow death to be gloomy all the time."

Today scientists tell us that that the physical action of smiling keeps us relaxed and healthy. Laughter lines make an old face beautiful too. A cheerful response to life and the tendency to see the funny side can keep us young and attractive whatever our age.

54

When we are old, the spirit within shines through, and the face tells all.

❝ When the truth shines out in the soul, and the soul sees itself in the truth, there is nothing brighter than that light or more impressive than that testimony. And when the splendour of this beauty fills the entire heart, it naturally becomes visible... Shining out like rays upon the body, it makes a mirror of itself so that its beauty appears in a man's every action, his speech, his looks, his movements and his smile. ❞

ST BERNARD

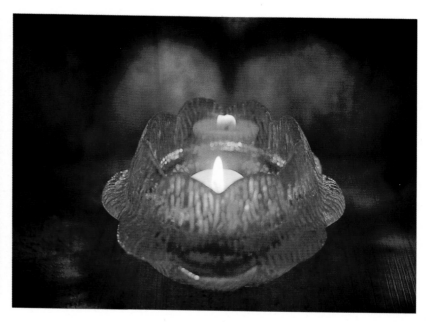

Light in the Darkness

"Do not seek death. Death will find you. But seek the road which makes death a fulfilment."
DAG HAMMARSKJÖLD

"Our God is merciful and tender.
He will cause the bright dawn of salvation to rise on us
and to shine from heaven on all those who live
in the dark shadow of death."
FROM LUKE 1

Many think of old age – like winter – as a time of fading light and gathering gloom. But, although our senses and faculties may grow dim as we grow older, the life of the spirit can burn more brightly as life goes on.

Jesus claimed to be the light of the world. Many have experienced his power to banish the shadows of sin and bitterness and despair. His closeness lights up the dark corners of loneliness and fear.

Death is often compared to the dark night.

It signifies final darkness to those who believe that we cease to exist when our bodies die.

For others, the blackness describes uncertainty and fear of what lies beyond death.

Death is darkness, too, for those who deliberately turn away from Christ, the Light.

The Christian picture of death is not nightfall but dawn. Death

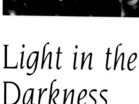

"The bright day is done
And we are for the dark."
SHAKESPEARE, ANTONY AND CLEOPATRA

56

heralds the light of everlasting day. Jesus conquered death when he rose from the grave.

He offers life to us all when he promises:

"Whoever believes in me will live, even though he dies."

A friend recorded her dying father's words. He murmured:

"When I go in to see the King it will be bright, very bright. It's all gone, all my sins, all my fears... only Christ now... I'm the happiest man alive... it's all bright, all bright!"

For some, however, the brightness grows dim when death is close. Towards the end of his book, *The Pilgrim's Progress*, John Bunyan describes his pilgrims as their turn comes to cross the river of death. Some are happy and triumphant; others, such as Christian himself, are full of fears. But all alike come safely to the city which shines like the sun.

" May all in whom the light of faith shines dimly, see at last. "
ST THÉRÈSE

" Though I walk through the valley of the shadow of death, I will fear no evil, for you are with me. "
PSALM 23

" May the Lord Jesus Christ, who is the splendour of the Eternal Light, chase far away all darkness from our hearts, now and for evermore. "

" God is light. "

" With you is the fountain of life; In your light do we see light. "
FROM 1 JOHN AND PSALM 36

Order of Bravery

*" I believe in the sun, even if it does not shine.
I believe in love, even if I do not feel it.
I believe in God, even if I do not see him. "*

WRITTEN ON THE WALLS OF THE WARSAW GHETTO

" Only now, in old age, afflicted by several chronic diseases, do I realize what it means to move constantly along the verge of exhaustion; to feel irritable because of sheer physical fatigue. " ARTHUR KÖESTLER

" We fix our attention, not on things that are seen, but on things that are unseen... So we are always full of courage. " FROM 2 CORINTHIANS

" In the old days, Death was always one of the party. Now he sits next to me at the dinner-table: I have to make friends with him. "

DAG HAMMARSKJÖLD

Courage is not the preserve of youth. It is the old who set an example of bravery. Yet most of us never even notice, beforehand, what it costs the older generation to live serene and self-sufficient lives.

Many of us, when we are old, need great physical courage. Pain may be a constant companion, by day and night. Ordinary chores become obstacles in an assault course when joints are stiff and sight and hearing are impaired.

Courage of mind is needed too. Many are left widowed after long years of marriage. Or it may be that a brother or sister or lifelong friend who shared the home dies. Loneliness is hard to adapt to for the first time at this age.

" Loneliness is a devil... So the message is loud and clear: keep going right up to the limit of your capacity all the time. " LORD RHODES, AT 92

Living alone brings its own crop of fears – the fear of intruders, or of sudden illness or accident, with no one at hand to help.

Courage is needed to face the future. Many of us wonder, "What will happen when I can no longer manage alone? What if my mind goes or my body needs constant care?"

Yet in spite of so much to cause frustration and dismay, many older people are cheerful and outgoing, interested in others and the world around. They cope with their disabilities without fuss or self-pity.

Some add to their courage a calm confidence in God, based on experience. They know that their inner spiritual life is being

renewed daily and that Jesus Christ, the source of their strength and peace, is with them whatever may come.

❝ As they came near to the village to which they were going, Jesus acted as if he were going farther; but they held him back, saying, 'Stay with us; the day is almost over and it is getting dark.' So he went in to stay with them. He sat down to eat with them. ❞ FROM LUKE 24

Growing in Secret

" God says: I like youngsters. I want people to be like them. I don't like old people unless they are still children. I want only children in my kingdom; this has been decreed from the beginning of time.

Youngsters — twisted, humped, wrinkled, white-bearded — all kinds of youngsters, but youngsters... I like them because they are still growing, they are still improving.

They are on the road, they are on their way.

But with grown-ups there is nothing to expect any more.

They will no longer grow...

It is disastrous — grown-ups think they have arrived. "

MICHEL QUOIST

" For even the purest delight
may pall,
And power must fail,
and the pride must fall,
And the love of the dearest friends
grow small —
But the glory of the Lord is all in all. "

In winter time, when snow covers the ground or damp mist lies over the countryside, it is easy to imagine that all growth in nature has stopped. But we know that, beneath the surface, movement and life continue.

When we reach the winter of life we need not stop growing either. Ambitions will change and horizons shrink. But, as one psychiatrist put it, we need to know "how to renounce without having to resign".

One way to go on growing is to keep asking questions about the world around us. Our interests will be different. We may explore scientific discovery, natural history, or art and literature, as well as following world events.

" It is because of God that I am interested in the world, because he made me and put me in it. I do not see any reason why I should be any less interested in it now than when I was young... I do not understand what that means, to prepare oneself for death... death will come for me just as I am, and what happens to me will depend exclusively, as it will for all other men ... on God's mercy. "

DR PAUL TOURNIER

We need to ask questions about other people too and to be interested in their affairs. When we become totally absorbed in ourselves we stagnate.

Above all, we must go on asking the big questions about life and death and immortality. When our hearts are set on God, we begin to explore a relationship with him that goes on growing for the whole of life. Best of all, we can be certain that when life on earth comes to an end we shall grow into perfect knowledge and know God as he knows us.